snapshot·picture·library

PUPPIES

snapshot·picture·library

PUPPIES

FOG CITY PRESS

Published by Fog City Press,
a division of Weldon Owen Inc.
415 Jackson Street
San Francisco, CA 94111
www.weldonowen.com

WELDON OWEN GROUP
Chief Executive Officer John Owen
Chief Financial Officer Simon Fraser

WELDON OWEN INC.
President, Chief Executive Officer Terry Newell
Vice President, International Sales Stuart Laurence
Vice President, Sales and New Business Development Amy Kaneko
Vice President, Sales—Asia and Latin America Dawn Low
Vice President, Publisher Roger Shaw
Vice President, Creative Director Gaye Allen
Managing Editor, Fog City Press Karen Perez
Assistant Editor Sonia Vallabh
Art Director Kelly Booth
Designer Andreas Schueller
Design Assistant Justin Hallman
Production Director Chris Hemesath
Production Manager Michelle Duggan
Sales Manager Emily Bartle
Color Manager Teri Bell

Text Sonia Vallabh
Picture Research Andy Sir

A WELDON OWEN PRODUCTION
© 2007 Weldon Owen Inc.

Library of Congress Control Number: 2007936043

ISBN-13: 978-1-74089-639-9
ISBN-10: 1-74089-639-4

10 9 8 7 6 5 4 3 2

Color separations by Sang Choy International, Singapore.
Printed by Tien Wah Press in Singapore.

Puppies come in many different shapes and sizes. You see them almost everywhere you see people—in houses and cars, in the park, walking down the street.

Puppies are great friends and have become part of our way of life. Every year, more people are bringing home pet puppies!

Puppies are born
with their eyes
and ears shut.
They don't open
them until they are
two weeks old.

Before they are even six months old, puppies will learn a lot. Like how to make friends—with each other, and with you!

Puppies can have long hair or
short hair. Some have spots.
Some have big floppy ears.

They can be
white, black,
brown, or gold.
Some even
have flat faces.

A group of puppies born together is called a litter. Some litters have twelve puppies— or even more!

Puppies have very sensitive ears and noses. A puppy can hear and smell much more than a person.

For a puppy, every time is naptime. A puppy can spend up to twenty hours a day sleeping!

Puppies love to
chew on toys,
like a stick or
a bone…

...or your foot!

Puppies love to run around. They
run so much that they use up twice
as much energy as grown-up dogs.

Puppies love long walks, too.
Maybe these puppies would like
to go for a walk. Let's ask them!

When puppies let their mouths
hang open and pant, they are
using their tongues to cool off.

Puppies love to hide. But they also love to be found!

When they grow up, puppies can
help people in a lot of different ways.

Some puppies will grow up to be police dogs that help find missing people. Some will herd sheep.

Some puppies will grow up to be guide dogs that help people. Others will pull sleds over ice and snow.

But for now,
there is lots of
fun to be had!

Puppies explore
every place
they go…

…and they
are very good
at finding
new toys!

Would you believe
that this little
puppy is related
to the wolf?

Puppies can be our best friends.

They can become
part of our family.

Taking care of our puppies means giving them food and water, but also spending time with them.

It means talking to them,
and playing games.

Puppies have
many ways of
showing their love!
These puppies are
giving each other
a great big kiss.

No other animal is as
friendly to people as a dog.

Luckily, there are more than 800 kinds of dogs. And all of them start as puppies!

Who's ready
to play?

ACKNOWLEDGMENTS

Weldon Owen would like to thank the following people for their assistance in the production of this book: Diana Heom, Ashley Martinez, Danielle Parker, Lucie Parker, Phil Paulick, and Erin Zaunbrecher.